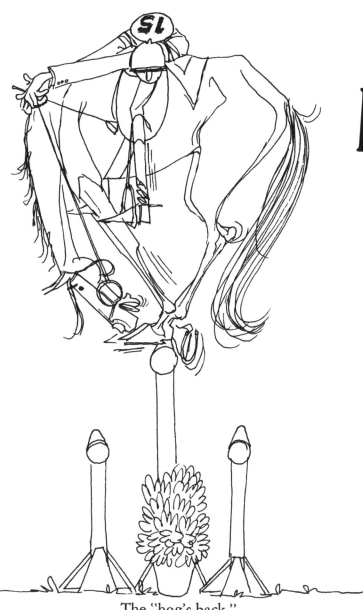

The "hog's back."

MUTCH ABOUT HORSES

MUTCH ABOUT HORSES

Cartoons by
RONNIE MUTCH

Introduction by
SAM SAVITT

The hunt breakfast.

THE LYONS PRESS
Guilford, Connecticut   An imprint of The Globe Pequot Press

60% performance, 40% *conformation???*

Originally published by Arco Publishing Company, 1978.

The Lyons Press is an imprint of the Globe Pequot Press.
Printed in Mexico
2 4 6 8 10 9 7 5 3 1

REMEMBERING OUR DAD

By Hugh C. "Bert" Mutch, Tori Mutch Eurton, and Christine Mutch Howell

Whether it was one of our birthdays, Christmas, or just a Tuesday, Dad's artistic talents embraced our lives. Our childhood bedroom walls came alive with hand-sketched hunt scenes in which the fox disappeared into the chest of drawers; Christmas and birthday cards were always drawn in his famous pen-and-ink style; and our home horse show courses at Nimrod Farm were sketched and painted in watercolor.

Dad always lived life through his creative eye. It is with great pleasure that we share with you just one of his many talents in this republication of MUTCH ABOUT HORSES. We hope you and your families will enjoy his unique outlook of the horse world as much as we do.

16½ couple.

MY FRIEND RONNIE MUTCH

By George H. Morris

Ronnie Mutch and I were personal friends and fellow professionals, our lives interwoven for the better part of fifty years. It began at the Ox Ridge Hunt Club in Darien, Connecticut. Victor Hugo-Vidal, Jr., Ronnie, and I were sort of the Three Musketeers, being the three junior boys riding out of Ox Ridge at the time. Victor was the brains, Ronnie the talent, and I the plodder.

In the early days many of us went down to White Plains to take lessons with Gordon Wright, reputed to be the best teacher in America, and he was! We went on the sly, because Miss Townsend and Otto Heuckeroth, the trainers at Ox Ridge, didn't like the idea. Then when Ronnie and/or his parents had a falling-out with Gordon, Ronnie moved to Al Homewood, the trainer at Boulder Brook in nearby Scarsdale, who was Gordon's nearest rival. Under Al's tutelage, Ronnie won the 1950 AHSA Medal Finals aboard a big handsome chestnut with a white face named Imperator. Ronnie's main junior horse at that time was a smooth gray mare named Left Aim. I can see to this day the pair sailing around outside hunter courses. Ronnie rode hunters beautifully. He had a great eye and lovely, quiet and soft hands.

1952 was my big year as a junior. We were at Madison Square Garden, and I had won the AHSA Medal Finals on Saturday, the first day of the big weekend. Then Sunday came along with the prestigious ASPCA Maclay Finals. I had a superstition about wanting to go first — I always went first and usually won (those were the days before independently drawn orders of go). Ronnie, who was some four years older than I was, was still in the Maclay, and for the afternoon round he and Glenna Maduro decided they'd go up to the In Gate very early and prevent my going first. I had my horse Game Cock trained so that if put my hand back on his croup, he would back and kick out. He cleaned that In Gate out fast! I slipped in to go first, and I won. Ronnie and I always competed like that—it was always one-upmanship.

When Ronnie went off to the University of Virginia, he started riding semi-professionally for many of the big owners and professionals. Ronnie was very close-knit with the Virginia horse community.

The big June show circuit in Connecticut was Greenwich, Ox Ridge, and Fairfield. The year was 1954 and I was out of the Junior Division. I had a new green jumper named Holy Smoke (I later changed his name to The Gigolo, which seemed more sophisticated and sexy). Ronnie helped me with the horse at the Greenwich show. The first morning he was warming me up for the rub class (in which touches counted). He had me jump a triple-bar backwards against big sheep-hurdle wings. We all turned arse-over-teakettle, as they say. I went down, the horse went down, and the whole fence went down. Ronnie picked up the pieces, put me back together, sent me into the ring, and we won. Unfortunately, my mother was driving into the show just as I turned over, and she saw the whole thing—I'll never forget how she wrung Ronnie's neck.

In 1955 Ronnie had a short stint with the fledgling civilian U.S. Equestrian Team at the Fall Circuit shows. Before he graduated from UVA in 1956, he paved the way for me as a freshman at that great country club of a university. He got me into the polo fraternity Chi Psi, as well as introducing me to others in his crowd.

Ronnie was always an extremely gifted artist, delighting people with his paintings, drawings, and cartoons. This talent took him into the advertising business. In the early '60s, Ronnie was married to his first wife (Patti Paterno, the mother of Grand Prix rider Hugh "Bert" Mutch), living in New Canaan and working in Manhattan, and doing a little work with horses on the side. At that time I was working and living at Jessica Newberry's place up in Lake Placid. Ronnie really started me as a professional. He introduced me to Jen Marsden, whom he taught. She lived near Albany, so I'd teach her whenever I drove back and forth to New York City. In 1964 when I hung up my shingle in Armonk, New York, Jen was one of my first big stars.

Ronnie started getting back into the horse business full-time in the mid-'60s. He couldn't stay away. It was in his blood. By the late 1960s Ronnie had reestablished himself as a top teacher and top professional. He then married an ex-pupil and good friend of mine, Sue Bauer. Together they bought and built Nimrod Farm and started winning a lot of classes.

It was still the Victor-Ronnie-George Three Musketeers, and while we were still good friends, we were also strong rivals. We were the best in the country, we knew it, and we tried hard to beat each other. That was more or less the scenario into the early 1980s. At that time Victor had moved to California to freelance teach and judge, Ronnie had sold Nimrod to get into freelancing too, and I'd gotten out of hunters and equitation to concentrate on the jumpers. During the last fifteen years of Ronnie's life, we saw each other sporadically although we remained very good friends.

I will always remember Ronnie as an extremely attractive and talented guy with a great personality. That made him a great politician in the horse business and a formidable foe. Ronnie was an excellent and natural rider both on hunters and jumpers. He was a ladies' man till the end, and women loved him. Ronnie was a natty dresser and possessed great style. He was a colorful remnant of the old school, yet always hip and up-to-date. I will never forget Ronnie, nor will the horse world. Our lives never strayed far from each other.

Competition makes us better, and Ronnie Mutch made me better.

THOUGHTS ON MY BEST FRIEND

By Victor Hugo-Vidal

How hard it is to summarize a lifetime that was intertwined with mine for over fifty-five years, especially when it was that of my best friend. Especially when it was a life snuffed out much too soon, a life I just took for granted would last as long, or longer, than mine.

Ronnie Mutch, George Morris, and I were the unholy triumvirate that grew up together at the Ox Ridge Hunt Club in Darien, Connecticut. Our friendship started before our teen years, during the war years (that's World War Two) with gas and food rationing stamps. We were under the tutelege of Miss V. Felicia Townsend and Mr. Otto Heuckeroth. What influences they had on our early years, a second set of parents in those innocent times.

Bicycles were our mode of transportation then, and we rode them everywhere: to town to get advertising for the two horse shows we put on at the club (gas rationing meant no one could van horses anywhere); to visit friends; to go to stamp club or the movies (TV was in its infancy then); to a wonderful lake in which we'd swim and smoke (of course, we didn't have permission). Ronnie and I were like brothers because we were only children (lucky George had brothers and sisters). What a super time to grow up, Ronnie and I often reminisced as we compared pictures of our grandkids and boasted of our families. We always thought how lucky we were, we wouldn't have wanted it any other way.

That was exactly what happened the last time I saw Ronzo. We were judging together at The Oaks in California. Although we saw each other only once or twice a year when our paths crossed at horse shows, it was as though no weeks or months had ever parted us. That's what best friends are all about. I miss and yearn for it to keep happening, but in my heart of hearts I know it won't.

Those of us who were privileged to have known him were witness to his many talents: artist, teacher, advertising executive and illustrator, spellbinding raconteur, humorist, rider, judge — but above all a great person.

I miss Ronnie. I always will, but I carry a part of him always with me, and it makes me smile as he always did. I'm thrilled his cartoons and illustrations are being reprinted so that new generations can chuckle at incidents that might happen to all of us.

And I know he's up there looking down at us, and he is smiling too. Here's to you, Ronnie!

THE MUTCH LEGACY

by Judy Richter

My last serious conversation with Ronnie Mutch was about how proud we were of our students who rode with us years ago and now still ride well and run successful horse businesses of their own. We agreed that it was great fun to see them doing it our way, but better than we ever could now.

We were standing at the grand prix ring at Wellington, watching his son, Hugh "Bert" Mutch, jump around a Modified Jumper class. Bert, of course, heads the list of Ronnie's kids who have gone on in the sport and done well; Bert shows an impressive string of jumpers and trains some good riders as well.

Among the famous international riders who trained at some point with Ronnie are Jay Hayes, the Canadian Olympian; Laura Tidball Balisky, another Canadian Olympic rider; and our own Olympic Silver Medalist, Greg Best, who rode ponies years ago with Ronzo. Jeffrey Welles is at the top of his game, consistently winning grand prixes and training a group of top riders and horses as well. Both Laura O'Connor and Fred Bauer now enjoy considerable success in the jumper ring.

Anne Morris, another Nimrod Farm rider, has distinguished herself in the dressage world, while numerous well-regarded horsemen and horsewomen are brilliant hunter riders and trainers. These include Lyman T. Whitehead, Lainie Wimberley, and Sarah Hochschwender on the East Coast, as well as Peter Lombardo, who successfully migrated to California.

And so, coast-to-coast and indeed worldwide, Ronnie's riders are still making their mark. The legacy to our sport from R.W. Mutch is indeed more than much.

REMEMBERING RONZO

by Steven D. Price

Ronnie Mutch liked me to address him as R.W. He said it made him sound like a professor. That was the joke, because there was no one less professorial than R.W. Mutch. He was a fabulous teacher and, in his way, a very learned man, but there was absolutely nothing academic or stuffy about him.

Some dozen years ago, I finally convinced Ronzo (the nickname by which many — including himself — referred to him) to consider writing a riding manual. He decided the subject should be how never to miss another distance. On the sensible theory that if he could teach that skill to me he could teach it to any rider on earth, he invited me to spend a long weekend with him in Palm Beach.

Ronzo arranged for me to ride horses at the Polo Club's stable. The first day I found myself on someone's lovely amateur horse. Under Ronzo's tutelege I found myself riding far better than I usually did and, even better, understanding why things happened as they did.

The next day, when the amateur took her horse away to a show, I was given the only other available mount, the barn's sole schoolhorse, a stolid senior citizen named Lucky. The day was hot and humid, so Lucky and I spent most of the session sharing a patch of shade with Ronzo and listening to his equestrian theories.

Bright and early the next morning, Ronzo and I returned to the barn to try to put the theories into practice. We were greeted by an unhappy barn manager and weeping children. I'm here to ride Lucky, I reminded them. You can't, I was told, Lucky colicked and died during the night.

Sad as the news was, it was too good for Ronzo to let pass. Henceforth and forever whenever I reported on missing a distance (a not infrequent occurance in my efforts over fences) or any other less-than-magic moment in American horsemanship, he'd just drawl, well, it's all Lucky's fault.

Others remember Ronzo's accomplishments as a world-class horseman and teacher — in fact, one of his legacies is how he demonstrated that real horsemanship includes the ability to teach. However, I knew him best and admired him most for his artistic and creative talents.

Ronzo envisioned magazine and ad layouts the same way he judged horses and riders or analyzed a Grand Prix course. His mind's eye took in everything at once: individual elements and the entirety. He had an artist's eye. You can't learn that: you're either born with that eye or you're not, and Ronzo had it.

Ronzo's cartooning was part of his personality. It took him only a few strokes to capture the essence of his subject. His wit could be as sharp as the tip of his pen or as gentle as a fine brush, but it was always right on the mark.

I'll remember Ronzo for that creative genius — the effortless flair and grace with which he created drawings, paintings, magazines and catalogs. Not that Ronzo didn't work at what he produced, and work hard, but like one of his memorable hunter trips the result always came out looking effortless. And it always looked right.

The French have an expression: Style is the man. That's the way I'll remember my pal, R.W. Mutch. He was a stylish guy, and not just in how he rode horses or wore clothes. He was the embodiment of a truth that's too often forgotten: fashions change, but style endures.

We are indebted to The Lyons Press for republishing this book. Although it will delight those who remember his talent and will introduce him to a new generation, I can't help regarding the republication with the bittersweet realization that Ronzo's untimely death prevented the appearance of *Mutch About Horses*, Volume Two.

Judging the hunter.

"Must stand gently for mounting and dismounting."

"Two yanks and a cluck."

"Horses will jump fences which simulate those most commonly found in the hunt field."

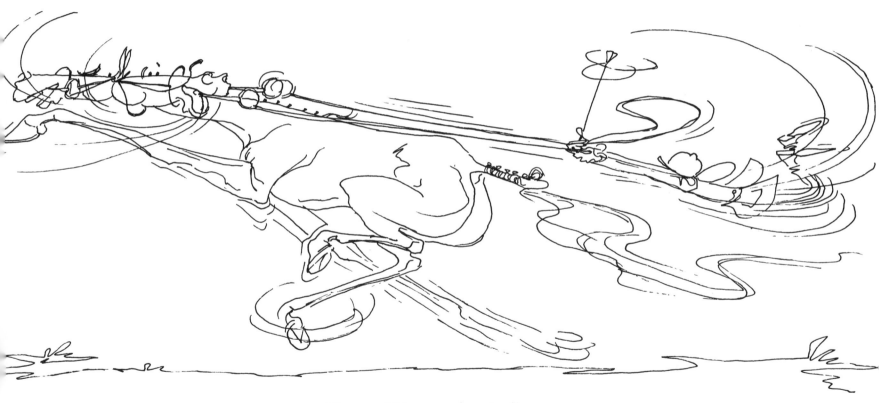

Horses will be moved on the line . . .

Hunter courses include chicken coops, in-and-outs, post-and-rails, etc., etc.

The "square oxer."

The "wishing" well.

A waiting distance.

The in-and . . . *out!*

"Looks like a nice *flowing* six."

"Due to inclement weather, appointments have been waived."

Distance 720 yards / Time allowed 1 minute 30 seconds / Water temperature 60°

Knocking down "timers"—*four faults*.

One fault.

Knockdown with any portion of horse or rider—*four faults*.

Failing to complete the course within the time limit—*elimination!*

Jumping an obstacle not included in the course—*elimination!*

Showing the horse an obstacle—*elimination!*

"In the fastest time *but . . .*"

"Narrowing the width of a spread without altering the height of any element which establishes the height is not considered a knockdown."

Quite often a light tap with a pole
teaches the horse more respect for fences.

No "scope."

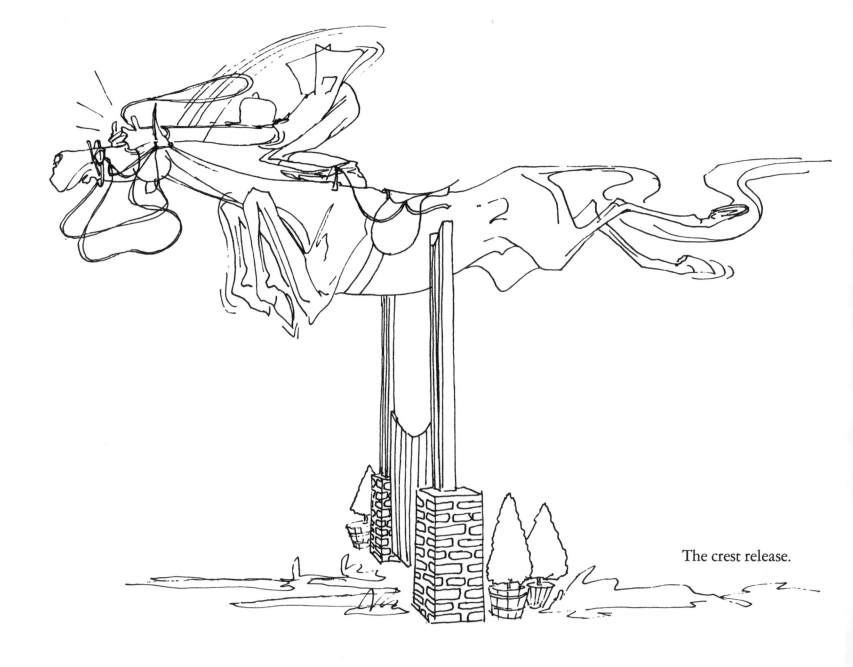

The crest release.

Gymnastics.

The triple bar.

"Somewhere out there . . . there *must* be a distance."

Two-point contact.

THE EXTENDED TROT

SHOULDER IN

PIAFFE

Dressage.

A real "daisy cutter."

"Herring-gutted."

Posting behind the motion.

The indirect rein of opposition.

Light contact is recommended.

Turn on the haunches.

Looking for the diagonal.

Stopping on a bending line.

Properly flexed, hocks well underneath, and . . . *halt!*

The pros and *cons* of the standing martingale.

Behind the bit.

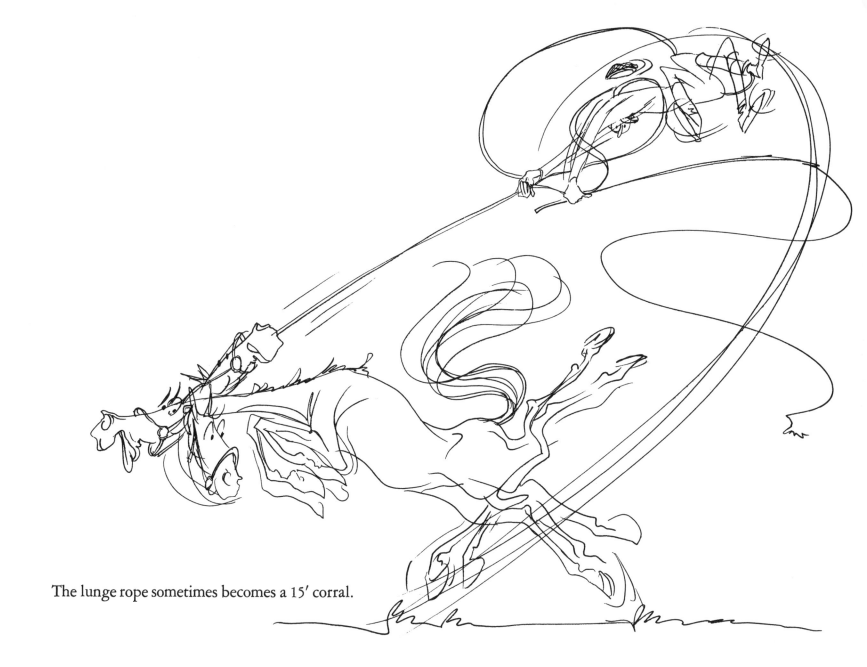

The lunge rope sometimes becomes a 15′ corral.

SHOULD BACK EASILY...

OPEN BRIDLE PATH GATES....

AND LEAD OVER SMALL FENCES !!!

The hunter hack.

"Casting" the hounds.

A handy hunter.

"Trappy" country.

A "safe" hunting distance . . .

Earning your colors requires a good knowledge of the country.

"Rolling" country.

"One or two strides?"

The stock tie.

The hunting breastplate.

The "stirrup" cup.

" 'Ware hole!"

Three-day event.

Roads and tracks.

The "grave."

The vet check.

Cross-country!

The "splash."